Love
DISCOVERY, RECOVERY, AND RELAPSE

MWIKALI WORDS

outskirts
press

Love: Discovery, Recovery, and Relapse
All Rights Reserved.
Copyright © 2017 Mwikali Words
v2.0

The opinions expressed in this manuscript are solely the opinions of the author and do not represent the opinions or thoughts of the publisher. The author has represented and warranted full ownership and/or legal right to publish all the materials in this book.

This book may not be reproduced, transmitted, or stored in whole or in part by any means, including graphic, electronic, or mechanical without the express written consent of the publisher except in the case of brief quotations embodied in critical articles and reviews.

Outskirts Press, Inc.
http://www.outskirtspress.com

ISBN: 978-1-4787-8236-0

Cover Photo © 2017 Mwikali Words. All rights reserved - used with permission.

Outskirts Press and the "OP" logo are trademarks belonging to Outskirts Press, Inc.

PRINTED IN THE UNITED STATES OF AMERICA

Gratitude and Love- A dedication

This work is dedicated to those who I have loved and who have loved me. This work is dedicated to those who have read my words and have heard my dreams and have said, "Go forth, You must." I thank you. Thank you to those who believed and waited and saw something worthy in the words. You know who you are. You have sent me forward and invested in my dream through your encouraging words and unexpected deeds.

This work is dedicated to the hurts we bear and the highs we feel when journeying to and living in the love. This work is dedicated to you, the reader, in hopes that love will find you and keep you and hold you...together.

Contents

Genesis 1

Discovery   3

The Best Laid Plans... 5
Diving 6
Singing 7
Communicating 8
On Taking Your Name... 9
Neat, Sweet and Funky 10
Conversational Kiss 11
Oceanic 12
Once Upon a Balcony 13
Hobby 14
Silence of the Lamb 15
Type 18
Sweet and Salty 20
Haiku Color Blue 21
Rubber Bones 22
Breakfast in Bed 23
Broken Healer 24
No Lie 26
Naked 27
You Play Me 28
he is of a cruel beauty 30
Words of Wisdom 31
How you like that? 32
Thrown 33
I'll Fly Away 34
Repentance 36

Mango Memories 37
The Not Forgetting... 38
Inhale: Intoxication/Love 39
He Loved Me Once 40
Loss 43
Memory Loss 44
These Are of You 45
Babel 47
The Power of the Tongue 48
Request 50
Atheist 52
There has been worship 54
Love Thyself Anyway 56
Thought it Might be Nice 57
Sense and Sense/ability 58
Hallucination/ Salvation 60
What am I Supposed to Do with All This Love? ... 62
Locked and Free 63

Recovery   65

Medicine Man 67
the fever breaks 69
Muscles 71
This Loving Thing 72
Finding Myself 73
I Should Get to Keep Him 75
I Don't Believe in Love Anymore...Again 76
For Vivian Green 77
For Saul Will I Am (And So You Are) 78
For Sunni Patterson Because She Rocks
    My Mental Space 80

Thoughts after an Evening on the Phone with Him .. 82
His Smile 83
In the Morning 84
Cream 84
Prayer 84
Running with You 85
Humming 86
The Agreement 87
The Simple Things 88
He Moves 89
Nervous System 90
Hunger and Satisfaction 91
Emergency 92
nina 93
You Have Me Listening to Music Again 95
Stuttering/Speechless 96
Naming Ceremony 97
By Heart 98
Naming Ceremony II 99
Pen-less Poet 100
Willing Addict 101
Traffic Light 102
Under Street Lights 103
Better 104
Restraint 105
His Hands 106
Breathing 107
Journey to Healing 108
Hoarders 109
Crazy 111
Lovely Again 113

Tears for You 114
Manipulation 115
Reminder 116
Skin 117
Longing 118
Lashes 119
It's There 120
Found Out 122
The Words 123
Everything 124
Time Enough 126
The First Time 127
Attempt at Excavation 128
Deadline 131
Substitute 132
California Closets 133
You Rock my World 134
Intelligent 135
The Way He Loved Her 136
Scars 138
I. 139
II. 139
III. 139
Allegory of the Cave 140
Anonymous 141
Easy 142
Prayer: I come to you 144

Relapse 145

Relapse 147
In Darkness 149
Glutton 152

Something Sweet	153
Dentist	153
Remodel your Mind	154
Massage My Mind	155
Honest	156
Flower Words	157
Wings	158
Needwanting	159
Sunbit (Just before Winter)	160
Sun Child	161
Dimples	162
He Comes to Me Quietly	165
Digestion	167
Journey Out of Mind	168
Since Yesterday	169
Pagefright	170
Claustrophobia	172
Mother and Son	173
If only you knew	174
He	175
Horror Story	176
Advice	177
Getting Over	179
Recovery and Relapse	180
Into the Air	182
be you...even in love	184
Tried Being an Ocean	185
Lesson	187
Discovery: Treasure After All	188
Prayer	189

Genesis

In the beginning was the Word
And the Word was with God
And the Word was God
And God is Love…

This is the story of a journey into finding the words
For the Love.
This is the story of the way she first began to know Love
This is the story of her worship
And her addiction.
This is a story of births and deaths
Beginnings and endings
This is a story of pilgrimage and passion
Of broken things and things everlasting…
This is a story of sin and salvation
This is a story of Love in all its omnipresence.
This is where it began,
Where it went,
And where it may yet go.
This is the Genesis of her Revelations
On Love.

Discovery

The Best Laid Plans…

She hadn't meant to give him everything
She had meant to save herself
For someone who *meant* the love.
She had meant to do the right thing…
The wait –for- a- ring thing…
But there had been tickling and temptation
There had been movies at midnight
And there was conversation and cuddling
There had been laughter that made it *feel* like love

And she had been convinced that if God is Love,
Then surely He would understand why…
Why when she felt this brand new, thick love for him
Him with the easy laugh
And quick tongue,
Why she would want all of him
Inside of all of her…
And waiting seemed more of a sin
Than inviting him in.

Diving

He tastes like the sea
And I'm always trying to remember
To breathe in the deep end.
I dive in.
Knowing the limitations of my arms and legs and strength in waters this deep...
I dive in.
I dive in because the love is on purpose
I dive in
Believing that the treasure beneath the surface of you will make it all worth it...
I dive in.

Singing

I sing in this love
Sing the parts I know
Hum the parts I don't understand.
Hum until I can find all the words for the music
Hum until the lyrics make sense in my head
And not just my heart
Hum against your neck
Hoping you can feel my music
Hoping you can dance to this beat
Hoping you can ride this rhythm
Hoping you can help me with this auditory art.
I sing in this love
Sing the parts I know
Hum the parts I don't yet understand.

Communicating

He lays me down beneath his laugh and
I'm held down with the weight of my amusement
This is our kiss
"Hello" and "Greetings" begin it
Our kiss
Between "hello" and "goodbye"
He slides
Between my cheeks and pulls slightly in to initiate
My dimples
His fingers play lightly at the edges of my stomach
He blows on my belly and
The muscles in my body tighten and release
Holding on till having to let go of
Laughter
Sometimes messy…
Often not very neat/together/pretty,
But always beautiful
He enters me with smiles and leaves me warm
And stretched inside
Making room for all that…
Personality
He elevates me
And I feel lifted and not lost at all
Just over all the shit I was tripping off of before
He enters me and stays awhile
And Lonely becomes a foreign tongue I no longer speak.

On Taking Your Name…

They say one of the most beautiful signs of love and commitment
Is the giving of a name
And hence, the receiving of a name
So what will it mean if I take your name
Just take it
For myself
Because I love you
And because you've
Changed me
Rearranged my mental and heart make up
Because you have taught me love language
And I speak it and write it everywhere
If I take your name as my own…
Is that marriage?
Will God recognize this thing we've made?
Is it enough?
Can I take your name
And say it
Or scream it
When the love reminds me of this
Rebirth?
Will that make it alright that I couldn't wait
To have you?

Neat, Sweet and Funky

I dreamt a dream of you in the morning
And your breath was funky
But I ...I embraced your kisses
I embraced you
I liked you ...*any* way
I pretended that you was a sweet treat
Acted like I was a neat freak
And folded you up
And set you on my lap
I folded you up and put you in my pocket
I folded you up and put you into my dresser
I folded you up and put you
Into me
Sweet and sweat and funk all
I wanted you
Any, and <u>all</u> the ways,
That I could have you.

Conversational Kiss

Beautiful how he hears me before and after he speaks
And we pack weeks between "hello" and "goodbye"
Our kiss
Our kiss 'cause we both use both our lips
We get inside each other
And I swear we find each other wet
And not caring about the rain
Or the time
We find each other at the gate
And I...
I can't say for him like I can for me
But me?
I...
I hold on for dear life (him/us)
Life/ Breath
After a while,
I thought they were both the same.
I hold on
And smile
And shake with the beauty of our laughter
Our kiss.

Oceanic

Give me seashell songs
Let me hear the rise and fall of us
May there be waves and foam to change the landscape of
What was.
May we have depth and be drenched
May we be oceanic and unapologetic

Once Upon a Balcony

I loved him too much
Loved him so much that I was becoming someone else
Someone with the potential to be the best and worst of me
Someone who couldn't take mocking laughter
And joking words about a possible other woman...
Someone who could push a Cali dude
Over a 6th floor balcony
Into an Atlanta night
And almost have to regret giving him this type of flight.

Hobby

I can't be your hobby
What you do for fun
You need to treat this relationship like a career
You need to work on it with your head down and
Eyes focused
Put in overtime when necessary
And you just might get a raise
And appropriate praise for a job well done
But slacking off just might get you laid off
Last pay check paid off
Might have to send you on an extended vacation
With no business or personal relations.
Just you holding onto a pink slip and memories
Begging on bloody knees and
I would hate to see you on the outside looking in
All because you gave pain and watched while I took it in
Watching the vacant position in my heart become
occupied
Learning that your application for a second chance has been
Denied
It's kind of late, but at least you tried?
It's a most unfortunate goodbye but,
Please don't cry.
Dry thine eyes
Go look for that greener grass you thought was on the
Other side.

Silence of the Lamb

Silent lamb on the altar of his love
Slowly licked by red-orange flames
Seared and moaning pet names
Cool steel penetrating soft flesh
Drawing out red reward
Continuous ceremony
Stealing sighs from wetted lips
Soft, barely breathing breaths erratically escape
He enters and exits with ease now
Lips curled in curious pleasure at the clear white she bleeds now
She is no more she
She is personified Relief
She is his deep mint-laced breathing in the night
Nevermore retaining her own identity
She cries for loss
Sighs for loss
Says too quick goodbyes to loss
Many nights of turned off lights and
She forgets she liked green grass
She relearns her preferences and concerns
She learns to like plastic turf
And forgets the smell of fresh green earth
She forgets the taste of living springs
And thirstily gulps at tepid puddles of muddied waters
Time goes by and her amnesia persists and
He insists that she wants what she hates

That he cannot be replaced
And she believes that he'll get better
So she waits
Anticipates a better he,
While she, goes on an emotional fast
Midnight snacking on the past
Thinking about when he used to...
And the way he used to...
Do what he won't do no more
She licks fingertips clean of flashbacks of him and her
And pure laughs.
She's so thin now
She barely grins now
Still...he bleeds her of her milky sustenance
While she inhales swirling air hugged in his scent
Barely breathing
Sill believing he will love her
Later
She lets her heart be a Benedict Arnold
Traitor to her mind
She goes insane
Pressing Stop and Rewind with her thoughts
Trying to find the part in the story of her life
Where he loves her
Foolishly fast forwarding fantasies of white gown and flowers
And sweet icing covered cake towers
Licking her lips clean of imagined cake crumbs
Humming along with mute dum dum du duuuummmss

Relationship striving on this insanity
Planning her life around who he plans to be
Until time and tears tornado earthquake shake her awake
And reality tastes bitter,
But more real than the fading sweet of imaginations
So she leaves the Eve in her and fights temptations
She wipes her eyes of fairy tale dust and
Foolhardy trust in
He who was just in *like* with her
And never in love
She loves him still
Silently
But now, she more readily
Learns to steadily love the she that she is
And the she that she is becoming
She is me learning to never sacrifice me to any "he"
She is me recognizing responsibility to love and respect
Me.
No more silent sacrificial lamb displays
Cause my heart is too valuable to be served on trays.

Type

He touched her in the night
And in the waking morning
Covered her body in caress
But couldn't picture her in white dress
He enjoyed her in hot showers
But couldn't see her throwing bridal flowers
To friends at no reception
Just his night time tickle...giggle...trickle...
Just a friend
His personal superwoman
Friend by day
Lover by night
But never a forever hold tight type
Just a turn off the light type
Wet and right type
Lover by night light
But he couldn't see his nighttime lady in a wedding ring
Couldn't see making a home...doing the Rockaway
Bedding thing
He only associated her with squeaky bedsprings
But sometimes she said things
That made him think she may want to be loved more than
Blockbuster and brown body bonds
She wanted the two kids and a dog
She wanted a house and a lawn
She wanted dinners together

She wanted to wake up to him in the morning and
Go to sleep to him at night
She wanted him to make nighttime right
Honest, pure
But he still wasn't sure he could do the marriage thing
The babies in a carriage thing
At least...he wasn't sure.... with her.

Sweet and Salty

Brown sugar breasts
In between breaths
He licks hardened brown sugar drops

He likes the tease to his taste buds
He likes it
Likes them
Likes him *in* me
But not him *with* me
And that's how he makes my face a salty treat.

Haiku Color Blue

Chewing a pen
I begin to drink blue ink
And eat all my words.

Rubber Bones

Rubber bones
Rubber bones
Make me fall so high
And touch the sky
And make it fall
On me

Breakfast in Bed

He came for breakfast
For some scrambling of eggs
For some long legs
Some buttered grits
Some plump tits
Some crisp strips of bacon
Some makeshift love makin'

And he said he'd be back for dinner
But he never came back
He left after he got full and fat
And satisfied
Gratified his hunger
That was winter
This is summer
And all I'm left with are memories of
The echo of
The echo of
The echo of
His belch.

Broken Healer

He came to me wounded
Dripping life wine all over my carpet
And I try and shout it out
Or something like that...
I make myself a receptacle for his pain
And sometimes it hurts
But I wince and take it and
Understand
When he pushes me as open as he can get me,
I cry.
I know he is hurting inside him
Like I am hurting between me.
I bear it like a mother
Pushing through.
Screaming sometimes
Groaning sometimes
Dealing with the tearing and the ripping,
As he tries to enter my womb
And feed off of my life.
It makes me hungry
Leaves me wanting.
With not enough left of me
To keep *me* full.
I growl inside
I push him back out into Life,
Covered in me
And all I have to give.

Nourishment.
I wipe him off
And send him back into the world
Strong and Walking
And better.
All better.
Renewed, refreshed
And letting the scab grow over the wound
Until...like a curious child,
He picks at it
To remember what his pain looks like
Under my cure for him.
I worry...but ...he'll make it.
The scab will grow back each time
I'll always be there taking him into my empty womb
And returning him to the world again and again
Me, torn and open and bleeding between my heart.
How will I heal myself
Every time I break myself
For him?

No Lie

Stupid ...
It's stupid how we lie to each other.
He says he misses me or has missed me.
It's been a month since we've seen each other.
I wonder if he misses me because he thinks that's what I
Need to hear.
I don't need to hear that.
I don't need to be missed.
Forget me if you're going to forget me.
Fuck the falsities and forget me.
Let the lie be free as an afro...
No Lie

Naked

He was so beautiful to look at
So beautiful to watch
I want to get over him
He finds the tension beneath his fingers
And pushes and pulls out the uneasy
He finds me and moves me around and
Under
Leaving me too sensitive...
Open...
Vulnerable to every word he says
Every possibility he proposes...
Naked
Naked and vulnerable
Naked and not strong enough fight the love.

You Play Me

You play me
Musician that you are
You play me
Strum my strings
Make music of silent things
You play me percussion
You play me with lust and
Maybe-love
Love…
You press your fingers in chords and runs
Didn't know I owned drums
Till you were drumming
And the sound was of me
Didn't know I was part guitar
Till you were strumming
And I was acoustic
You make music out of me
That makes *you* lose it
And you're dancing between the breeze passing between
The swaying of my hips and the rise of my knees
And I croon night songs
I bend the air with my lips
Saxophone…trombone
I am making the air my own
Moan
Music
See bop bop shu weeeeeee

How you've got me in all genres of sound
And it goes down in
Deep bass beats
You play me sweet
And I was bound
To hit some high notes

he is of a cruel beauty

He is of a cruel beauty
He knows his power and would
Press a lady heart against itself
With the pressure of his thumb
And his face would stay a stone beautiful
And she would plead with her eyes
And he would crunch lady bones
Between the strength of his
Beautiful teeth
And let her neck be a resting place for his
Beautiful feet
She would push her fists against his chest and he would
Calmly reply,
"That's not a lady-like thing to do."

Words of Wisdom

Never beg
I must remind myself of the words my mama spoke to me
Never beg for anything
Beg no man
Nothing of flesh and blood is to be begged
I think I must add that to the list:
Don't get too happy.
Don't breathe too easy.
Don't put high hopes in humans
Don't let them take it from you.
Don't beg.
Be your own person...
Independence is oxygen.
Don't place your hopes or your happy thoughts with
*any*One.
Don't let anyone feel the soft parts.
I have to remind myself at all times...
Don't let them touch where blood flows.
Don't let them inside the softness.
Don't let them inside throbbing veins where life flows
Because that's just...
Too close.

How you like that?

Night and slippery limbs
Rock hard
His thighs were rock hard
As he danced between my thighs
And swung his locs in the air
Dark chocolate ...
His skin...coffee...straight...
Keeping me awake
All night
Knees burnt from the impact...
Out of control...
No love... just fuck
How you like that?

Thrown

She would throw herself out if she could
She would throw herself out with both arms and both feet...
She would...
She has tired herself and is not getting enough sleep
She is finding herself and losing herself ...
And the events of both categories are occurring much too close together...
The floor is wet.
She is sliding...
She falls...
She breaks both knees and the progress has paused and perhaps stopped indefinitely
There is fear and hope and panic and passion and
...and... please...and please...please
Let her have her one moment of magic
Please let there be more than that hug...that touch...that fuck
Let there be more and more and more and let her be ready to receive...
And feed her so she believes in food and full/satisfied
She would throw herself out
Of her own self-doubt
If she could
She would throw herself out with both arms and both feet...
She would.

I'll Fly Away

I'll fly away
I'll fly away…like happiness and not like a threat.
I'll fly away like happiness
Like divine closeness or closeness to divinity
Keeping away all the bad
All the bad that I forgot was bad for a while
I remember now that others and I suffer because of bad me.

I crawl in my mind.
Crawl towards the altar
The altar promising better things and cleanliness and goodness.
I wish for magical waters to wade in
Magical waters that wash away all the bad
Magical waters that I fall in
And when I rise again
I've left my bad twin behind and
Drowning in holy water
And I…
Rise victorious
(Clean)
I raise/lift/ elevate my voice to Our Father,
Who resides in Heaven
Till I'm hollering out His name

I keep wanting to be rescued …to be changed
Father, forgive me for my foolishness

I think I've sworn off fire water...
I'm giving up fire water
'Cause it burns up my brain
Every time...
And someone gets hurt...me or others...or both...
Someone gets hurt always...
Every time I dip my brain in gasoline
And light a scented candle...
Leaving the air smelling like burnt black berries
And ashen skin and
Wine.

I cleanse my lips with Christ's blood
And cloak my insides with his flesh
Praying that I'll get better as I digest
And maybe this is how I'll heal myself
Tasting God
Maybe this is how the scab will form over the continuous flow of
Tainted blood
Tainted blood flowing from me
Tainted blood all over my knees,
Where the skin breaks

I lick my face clean of repentant libation and
Fall in prostration before my Maker
My Maker bigger than me
Bigger than me so small and petite beneath
His bronze feet
Heal me... I bleed.

Repentance

She was often repenting
For what love made her do
Often repenting for how she would suicide
To have the type of love that would
Take her breath away

Mango Memories

Mango nectar comes thick and smooth in my mouth
Easing and staying on my tongue and
I realize I don't want to be here....

Here
In the land of the free and the home of the brave
And the land that made slaves
In the land where Jim Crows flew bold
In the land where even after Malcolm and King and
Picket lines
And a new time...
It is still sometimes...much too hard to breathe...

Mango nectar reminds me
Of my aunt's front yard fruits in Kilifi
And I lick Mombasa from my lips and into my voice box
Saved for a song I'll sing later
In a foreign/native tongue
In a space that knows I belong
And am permitted my breaths.

The Not Forgetting...

I'm not forgetting and the loving is hard
The loving is hard and I can't bite through it
I can just lay on it
Or be crushed beneath it
Shattered teeth it...
I'm not forgetting
I am eating memories
I am a glutton and it's giving me gas
I am stinking from the loving and saying "pardon me"
I am asking forgiveness for what comes of the love...
Pardon me

I am swinging off midnight gates and landing on his chest...
I knock there...
He won't let me in...
He stands guard with a sword
And he smiles

My mind is midnight snacking on the memory of his eyes...
His smell...
Black and mild...

I am screaming my love for him between bites and am leaving holes in my phone.

Inhale: Intoxication/Love

I just want to love him
Swirls and swirls of him
Eating away at the insides of me
Making it hard for me to breath
I light him over my smoldering heart
Inhale him...
He keeps me warm and takes me high.
I cough when it's all too much,
But my lips won't deny me.
I drag him in...
Hold him in my lungs
And it becomes easy to believe
That loving him is like breathing.

After years of loving him, I realize the love is toxic.
After loving him so long,
I am charcoal inside
Charcoal and sunset colors.

After years of loving him,
I find my wish granted
He has taken my breath away.

He Loved Me Once

He held me once
Loved me once upon a time
Loved me in my front yard
No shame in the thing.
Bold.
My friend...my heart...my very heart...
He is the very heart of me
The very heart of me
Me ...heart amputee...my fault
Gone ...gone...gone...
My fault.
The heart of me...
Him who I loved
Like I've loved no other
Loved like almost drowning and
Gasping for air sometimes
Loved him like dreams of
Falling and falling
And never finding ground...
I fall still
Gasp still
For loving him
And whenever I hear a train blowing warning...
I think of traffic and laughter and us...
Train rides and free people and us
Broken flip flops, piggy back rides, and us
First time love, rice crispy treat eating us

Teddy bear sheets...jazz beats dancing us
Us so lovely
So meant to be
Us
Us so gone...broken...pieces of us...
Us...now?
Him over there and me over here...
My fault...
He was my heart...
My very heart
He was my heart and the beats in between and
We used to dance to us
I'll miss him
My heart and all that it held.
My tears
My sorrow
My memory
My happy thought: him...
Us...
My heart...
Our song...
I lay on the empty dance floor
Where our love had been a slow dance...
I lay on the dusty tracks of our leftover love...
And listen for the train that will take me away from what was.

Loss

He draws...
Knows about shading and toning...
An artist...
Him.
Plays guitar
Raps sometimes... (badly)
Sings in the bathroom
Gets too hot to hold me when he sleeps
Has lashes that remind me of butterflies
Laughs like magic and mischief.
Loves speed and the sound of revving engines
Craves year -long sunshine and sometimes, me.
But these...these are just patches of memory
It's over now and I'll miss the warmth of our hugs
I will miss the warmth of our us held together in conversation and laughter
Beautiful by the gates where I had been waiting to be more.
Waiting and not knowing that I was the *only* one who had fallen into this ...
Us.
Waiting until I couldn't wait anymore
Waiting and learning too late that when I had left
He had shed tears...too late
Now... I shiver
Now there are year-long blizzards...
Outside of an "us"
I stand outside of an "us"
Trying to cloak myself in memories of him.

Memory Loss

It is becoming difficult to remember him
All I can remember are his lips and hands
I am disturbed by this
I can't remember his eyes

Palm trees and sunshine
Black Dante
Gotta make the song cry...
Black and Mild
The pieces of him that linger

I write him down and
Wonder if one day he'll be at Borders
Flipping through, browsing...
And then there he'll be
Up against pages
And pages
Of my leftover heart.

These Are of You

I want to give him the poems.
He has to understand.

I want to say,
"Here, take these poems,
They are of you...
I made these poems of you...
You are their main ingredient
Take them, they're yours."

Babel

I had been trying to make a name for us, but
I could no longer understand you
Or you me
We spoke in different tongues
No amount of well-meaning kisses
Could bring us back to the basics.
I wanted to name us: "We"
And you did not agree
And called it a misnomer
And I called you:
Container of shit
Stinking of fear
And good for nothing but fertilizer
And, "I'm grown," takes on a whole new meaning
You grew me up and out of the love story
I had been writing
In a language, you could not understand.

The Power of the Tongue

Wet
Pink
Words easily slipping off
Passing easily like VIP through lips
The Words
Fluid....
Easily venomous or miraculous
Easily either
Just like that...either....
Just easing their way into the ear....
Layer by layer...floor by floor
Playfully playing on eardrums...disrespect or friendly gesture?
The Words
Knife behind back and smiling
The Words
Kissing and caressing
The Words
Duplicitous Words
Wearing Semantics and Memories
The Words
Breaking me in half.... willing me whole
The Words
Is the power in them or in the tongue they come from?
Or in the one who thinks them and sends them forth so quickly before they can be taken back...
Soldier words with guns and roses

Giving out wounds and windows and worlds
Wet
Cold
Too Hot
Too Raw
Too Much for right now when the bandages are still on...
The Words
The Tongue
The Altered Mind...
The No Rewind...
It all intertwines and amounts to a change that can't be undone....

Request

I want nice,
Clean pillowcase and purple sheets love
Love without the smell of mildew and stale coffee.

I'd like clear water love
And gray pebble love
Love like roasted marshmallows
Without the summer camp mosquito bites

Love, without used straws to sip it up with
Love without used lines
Used hands
And used eyes
"Don't use those eyes on me
When you don't mean
What your eyes are attempting to say."

I want tailored love that fits around the hips
And through the leg

I'd like unrushed,
Slow-cooked love

Hot and sweating love
Sweet and warm love
Baked crispy
With sticky sweet treat inside

Love without dust
Without lonely lust,
Missing the love parts...

I want love that eats the echoes
And burps them gone.

Atheist

All that's left are memories
And she's fast becoming an atheist
She once believed in Love
Now she hated it
Hates every February the 14th
Detests the color red
Changed her queen to a twin sized bed
There was a time when she bowed her head to Love
Closed her eyes and held Love in her dreams
Birthed Love
Pushed Love out and
Took Love in between trembling knees.
Bit into
Licked up
Sipped up
Digested Love.
Wrapped her arms,
Wrapped her legs,
Wrapped her mind
'Round Love
Opened her fists, her eyes,
Her time and thighs to Love
Devout believer
Loudest preacher
Fanatic follower of Love
Sharp like razors her Love
Soft as babies her Love

And there was blood.
Sacrifice, submission,
Suicide
(Couldn't count how many times
She died to She)
Worshipped "we"
Rug burned her knees
Choked on a Cali breeze
Poured lava from her lap
Turned her mind to sap
Hoping he would pour it over something
And taste her thoughts of him
And find them
Sweet
But he had consumed her
Had chewed her
And tried her
Had craved her
But when she called him hers
He denied her
And she is fast becoming an atheist
She once believed in Love
Now she hated it.

There has been worship

There has been worship
I have knelt and presented prayer to him
I have loved him and
Licked him
I have died five times
And he has not noticed.
In the face of resurrection,
I have sighed and been tired at the prospect of living again
And he has not noticed
He has *been*.
And the existence has been enough
And not enough
Enough
And not enough

I have cried and dried up with nothing left to give and he has not known.
He has loved my agony
And has not loved me and
I think maybe that's hate
Maybe he hates me
Penetrates me and
Laughs and
Leaves...and
He could be a tree with how much he leaves...

I am growing up to climb over the bullshit...
No jumping necessary
No jumping...
Strictly climbing
He is not love
He is therefore not God
And I will no longer worship there

Love Thyself Anyway

The disappointment doesn't end
She keeps trusting the trifling brothers
And learning too late that they were fake
Counterfeit companions.

So she turns to her own hands and
Dreams of good vibrations.
And consistent hands.
She howls at midnight
Howls at lunar loving and
Decides not to care about what was
She decides not to care so much about ancient, mistaken love
Not enough to starve herself of satisfaction

Instead, she will make him eat his words
Lick the consonants
Shape the vowel sounds
And when he burps,
It will stink of his lies.
And she will be satisfied.

Thought it Might be Nice…

Not sure if I know how to be loved
Thought about how nice it would be
To be massaged in the morning
With no particular agenda in mind
Just a simple desire
To touch with skill
The back and neck rub
Just because
Thought it might be nice
That's all.

Sense and Sense/ability

Kiss the back of my neck in the morning
Trace my tummy with your fingertips to wake me
If you will
Bite my shoulder sometimes
It's fine
Push your hands into the contours of my back
Wrap a leg 'round the rise of my hips
Mini Mt. Everest
Taste the smile on my lips
It will make you full
Hold my hand sometimes
Touch my face, carefully
Look at me with both of your eyes
And show me you're seeing me
I'd like to see me seen by you
Place your ear near my lips sometimes
So I can know you're hearing me
Feeling the warmth of my words
Nearby your mind
Hearing me
Rest your head in my lap
Feel my pulse
Understand the urgency
Hear the fire in my bones
Recognize the arsonist in you
Baby love, smell me
Sometimes I'm sandalwood

The aroma may make you hungry
Bon a petit
Eat me
Taste my travels
I've been on my way to you all along.

Hallucination/ Salvation

Recently found out that exhaustion causes hallucinations.
The mind creates pictures of what you *want* to see,
So as to save you the energy, that you don't have, to arrive at the place
Where said image would be in reality.
And this information/knowledge
Is making me rethink everything I used to believe in times of "love"
It makes sense now.

I was tired from the running,
Climbing,
Crawling after love
With no success and no end in sight
So...
So my mind, thinking she was performing a kindness,
Created these images/hallucinations of me being loved
And experiencing love things.
My mind worked overtime
To save my heart from too-deep sleep.
My mind *meant* well by these mirages,
But now I'm going back over memories and wondering
Where to file the hallucinations of hugs
And kisses and text-messaged love words
Where to file mistaken memories
Where to file the dreams I had
When my heart got tired.

And I have no answers yet
And I want to convey to my brain
The disservice it was to try and save me from reality.

The waking up places make sense now
After the rest, my heart awoke to the realities of this...
Mt. Man I'd been trying to climb into
And now it makes sense that his eyes
Were always laughing at me
(I had always thought it was just an overwhelmingly great sense of humor.)
Of course he'd be amused by me
Me thinking we were love.
In truth, I was just seeing moving pictures of my mind's sympathy.
My brains felt bad for me.

And he was laughing
Of course, he'd be laughing
The pictures had made a fool of me.
I was loving him off of memories
And staunch belief that
I could live in his chest
But instead, I awoke to being homeless.
Homeless and naked
Under a street lamp somewhere in Atlanta
Where it had finally been made clear:
He had been laughing at the absurdity of my unshaken belief in us.
And my mind is sorry for the mirage she had created.

What am I Supposed to Do with All This Love?

What am I supposed to do with all this love?
All this love with your name on it
What am I supposed to do?
Knowing/understanding there is no getting over you...
What do I do?

There is this thought that maybe it happened this way
Because I loved too much
Maybe it happened like this so I could get back
To me
Maybe when I've gotten my life together
And he's gotten his together too
Maybe then...
Maybe then I will have earned the right to the love.

There is also this me telling myself over and over in my head
Telling myself
Over and over
"He doesn't love you."
"He doesn't love you."
Thinking that enough of such thinking will alter my feelings.
It doesn't help.
I still love him.

Locked and Free

She locked her hair
To free her mind
Thought of doing something that could
Create a sense of
Permanency.
He had hated her "natural looks"
Bore with them with hopeful anticipation
For the straight, shiny look
The smell of burnt hair
Waited for that

Now that they were over
She separated her hair in sections and let them bond over time.
She did it because it was over
She did is so it would always be over
To seal the deal
Make it clear,
That now she would be who she had wanted to be
All along.

Recovery

Medicine Man

I came to him after the love had gone.
I came to him, knowing it would not be love.
I did not believe anymore...
Empty inside.
I came to him, to be cured.
And...
I feel healed with his hands parting me
Into two halves of foamy sea
Making way for him.
Miracle.
Dancing like moonlit African nights long ago
And I'm a tight beating drum
And he...
He is dancing piece of night sky
Dancing in a trance
Hypnotized by ancient rhythms and the smell of spice-filled air...
Dancing ...dancing
Stomach muscles tensed and hard in tight press...
My lips part,
Glazed in the molasses of his mouth
His hair hangs about his face
Ropes of patience and care
Smelling of shea butter and mango oils.
He wears my legs like regal necklace ...
Eyes droop in quiet fullness...
Filled with his rhythm and the sound of his breathing

I no longer feel empty.
He is healing me like this ....
Replacing ancient hurt with pain I can deal with
He is dancing passion fruit from me
And squeezing for more ...pushing for more...
Leaving me sure that this dance will cure me.

the fever breaks

I've been beaten
I've been beat about the head and against the ears
I've been kicked in the most vulnerable part of my stomach
And I've gone back
I've gone back and back and back and
I've been beaten
And gone back
And been beaten
And gone back because there was also the nice...
There was also the nice
The petting
The syrup words
And I've gone back
And licked the hand that beat me hardest
And gone back
And ate the leftovers thrown down to me
And gone back
I have...and have and have finally
Seen the bruises and scabs for what they are....
Bruises and scabs
I have finally seen the bruises and scabs and have stopped calling them memories...
I have finally seen that the lovely came in a temporary capsule and
Dissolved and
Wasn't good no more...

Expired...
Wasn't good no more
Was poison
Wasn't good no more
It took a shot of rememory to cure me
And it hurt
It stung...burned going in...
But it was good...
All better...good
And at last...
And finally ...
Seven years later...
The fever is gone.

Muscles

My desire for muscles
Has a lot to do with my desire
To rely
On myself.
No weak spots
Nothing pinch-able
Nothing like dough.

All marble,
Smooth and hard,
Unbreakable.
I want muscles
To make my skin hold tight to my strength,
And ripple over
My refusal
To bend.

This Loving Thing

I think that perhaps I've lost my mind in this
Loving thing.
Think I may have been soaking in it too long,
And I've got to work it out of me.

I've got to get back to the other parts of life
The music parts...
The art parts...

I need... Inspiration.
Something to believe in.
Something to remind me
What it's like to believe in something other than love.
Need to desire something more than love.
Love, which is nice...
But not enough.

Finding Myself

Do something
Do something...Please

I plead with myself
Find her...find her...please
Find her cause she's waiting and pacing
And placing all her hopes on being found
You ...you...you
Find her
Find her because she will save you.
Be brave you.
Summon all courage.
Call to your muscles.
Stand on your toes
And remember the promise in your
Calves.
Remember the meat of your legs
And all things kinetic
Waiting inside you with so much
Potential.
Find she ...
Find she will save you.
At the end of all days and nights
Behind the secret smile of
Every whispered sunset
And just about the rim of
Every wet sliver and ball of moon

There is sun.
There is you with all the possibility of a new day
Hungry for what's next
Bouncing on the ball of your feet
You
Find her, and she will show you
The parts you forgot.
And remembering,
Will give you Wings.

I Should Get to Keep Him

Damn it
I feel like I should get to keep him
Cause I love him lovely and
When I peek down my shirt,
He's there
Swinging his legs and
Smiling a little bit
And examining his hands.
He is.
And I feel like I love him and also want to keep him
Cause parts of me still warm with his
Leftover fingerprints.
Cause parts of my lips are still wet
With just the *memory* of his kiss.
I feel like I should get to keep that...
That damn heart of his,
Hiding deep behind his polo shirt.
I'm just saying
I'd like to save him
From the pain
Of seeing me too late.

I Don't Believe in Love Anymore... Again

I don't believe in love anymore.
I don't believe in love,
Like I don't believe I can fly.
Either belief can lead to a pretty nasty fall.
A fall in love...
A fall to the death...
Either way...
Some part of you leaves another part of you.

Fall in love... and your mind takes one side
And your heart, the other
And it makes living as just one you...harder.
Fall, with the belief that you have working wings,
And your spirit will leave your clumsy body in its new understanding.

I have found that I no longer have the desire to learn the truth of the fall.
Therefore, I don't believe in love anymore...again.

For Vivian Green

Sweet Miss Green
You see
Sweet, sweet Miss Green
With your long, and flowingest of skirts,
And the little curls atop your head and against
Your temples...
You are singing all the parts of my heart
I think about most.

For Saul Will I Am (And So You Are)

I read you straight through without stopping
Read you with partial understanding
Meant to stop longer
Meant to take smaller bites
Meant to, but found myself hungry
And open
And wet
(Drooling)
I read 2 worlds of you and wanted to be in both
I read you straight through
Finding I could not be stopped
Bit my lip when I saw my name on your pages
Even if you weren't talking about me
You were talking to me
And I guess this is all to say,
I'm hearing you
I hear you
Heard you
I'm hearing you (It will not stop)
I'm hearing you and am inspired
I shall not fear
I am re-fired to commune with my heart
And digest my mind
I'm hearing you
You've been heard
And I will be deciphering you over and over

And hungry
And open
And wet (Drooling)
Ready.

For Sunni Patterson Because She Rocks My Mental Space

Her voice is like djembe drum
Fierce, with the power to calm still.
I love her for her voice and its garments
Worn well down the red/pink carpet
And out through the lips of she.

She inspires me to be better in my times new roman, gel ink, pencil, chalk...or
Whatever is available when needed to make a message.
Makes me want to be healthy
And live long
And make the most of my lung's capacity and beyond...

She is beautiful young prophet,
Hair cut to make the brain shape mo' clearer
Massai-like loveliness...
I call her "my highness" 'cause she makes me take steps, elevators, and wings to the truth she speaks

She speaks...
In a Shaka Zulu song- type- way
In a pastor in the pulpit- type way
In a mama said-type way
In a grandma- knows- type way
In a truth -be- told- type way

And I love her and wish to learn her and sip at her cerebral,
Which is sweeter than palm wine
And runs further and deeper than the Nile.
She shakes her finger at the American denial of fault
And hugs those renamed survivors cause "victim" didn't
fit right over the muscles of them

And I love her...
Like I love the star she is named after...
I love her,
Hear her,
Draw near her
And come to the light...

Thoughts after an Evening on the Phone with Him

I walked the smile all evening
Before I reached the other
Side of his face
And found rest on his cheek.
After all the laughter,
I ate his face.
Chewed on a smile for a while.
It was tender.
Dined too on the angry/ sad parts
And chewed a long time,
Before I could swallow the sometimes defeated parts
Or the baked courage places.
The sweet layering of eager loyalty
And easy lovely
Left me blind for a while,
With my close-eyed smile
And I tripped on your dimple
On the way to your ear
And was amazed how well I fit in there
At the listening part of your face
Yes...feasted on your face
All night.
Digested your personality and
I do believe, when I was finished,
I rubbed my belly
And belched.

His Smile

I am enamored with his smile.
The biggest smile I've ever been acquainted with
The perfect set of teeth between necessary lips.
Long as several face miles...
I pilgrimage to his happy
And rest my knees on his adamant joy
And am made whole.

In the Morning

Do you know I woke to the sun
Thinking about your smile
And was satisfied?

Cream

Do you know I dip the tip of my finger
Deep
In memories of you
And come up with cream?

Prayer

Do you know, thinking of your smile
Makes me bow my head
Like prayer?

Running with You

We are excited about the pavement
We have vowed to pound together
The breathing we will need to be doing
The breathing in and outside of harmony
Next to each other
Breathing
Smacking the air down and out of the way
So we can travel through it
Anxious about the stretching before and after
The ankle touches
And head rolls
We are nervous and nice thinking about the way
Our skin is bound to diamond
Brown sugar diamond...
Running down the back of calves
Wondering when the water will be needed
To cool the oxygen coming hot and fast and almost
dangerous.
More than all things,
We are tight
And trying to hold the flying eagles together
In our bellies
When thinking about what all this
May do to our hearts.

Humming

I remember Dwele and Mahogany meeting
And Jill Scott's "Long Walk"
With him
I remember Common's questions
"What if God Were a Her?"
This is what love with him did.
The love made me remember a few of my favorite tunes.
The love made me hum
Without meaning to.

The Agreement

I don't want to acknowledge this love because
It seems too soon for me to be spreading my love like jam
And feeding it to him now...
Too soon.
I mean,
Me and Love...
We had an agreement...
Love was supposed to wait on me
So I could get my life together
Before I got my love together.
Thought we'd shook hands on that...
But now Love is threatening to push in.
Pull under my collar bone and settle in my chest.
Ready to leap on in...
And...
Maybe Love knows better than me,
And is showing me how I'm wrong
And how love is nice...
Whenever.

The Simple Things

He's excited about eating with me.
Tasting... at the same time.
He's excited about lunch or dinner or whatever else.
Says, he's never supped with someone like the way he wants to
With me
Said he doesn't really dress up much
But he would/ will for me
Said, "I'd do that."
Just like that.
And it means something to me.
I wouldn't require dress code,
But it's nice that he cares about the possibility that I might.
And we share words so nicely...
So nicely they come to my ears and I feel that I could be healing this way.
He makes it so important that I live so I can have another day with him...
And his safety is important to me too because
I want,
Each day,
Another day with him.

He Moves

He moves to the music left over in my mind,
After his smile.
That smile,
Those amazing teeth,
Those eyes...
Deep, deep brown...
The color of simmering love
Taking it's time.
I've decided his eyes are the color of
Patient love
And I jump in and hold my breath beneath his irises.

Nervous System

She roll she hips 'round his mind
And turn him thoughts to wine
She sip slow
And him slur him own speech
She champions his very mental working

He cannot walk in a straight line
Cannot talk with the full capacity of his mind
Cannot blink his eyes
For watching the magic of her thighs
Her savage sway will weaken his stance and
He will not remember what to do
With his hands

And damn...she face...
And damn...she waist..
And damn she takes she time
Tearing up he spine
And rewires
His entire
Nervous system...

Hunger and Satisfaction

He is making me hungry
I long for him...
My body earthquakes without him...
But he is also making me full...
Feeding me sincere words and tangible actions...
And I'm often biting my lip
And rubbing my belly
After having him.

Emergency

The lights were red and blue
And a white that seemed like yellow
Spinning 'round and 'round
Fast and urgent-like
The streets were the color of emergency
The night his hug came with the sweetest kiss.
Unexpected,
Welcomed
Kiss on my right dimple.
Color Purple: the feeling spreading through me....
The color of passion....
A welcomed urgency.

nina

Burn incense and let the ashes fall
Like your face
Like October leaves
Let there be no light...save the candles of melon, sage, tea...
Do not sleep
Think
Dip your head deep in the waters and give yourself a new name for the night
Be different
Appease
Please
Put a spell on a lover
Put your smell on a lover
Kick the covers off your bed 'cause it's summer
And too hot to be clothed in anything at all,
Save the smoke of burning incense and the thickness of the dark

Suck in smoke and watch the fires intensify
Lick the black/purple lips that are yours now
Swallow Nina....and you might find *night time is the right time for just reminiscing*
Touch Simone from the nape of the neck to the end of the spinal cord
And learn the story of strange fruit on southern trees...
And maybe this will ease the pain of change...

That was bound to come...
Sam Cooke said so...but you never quite see it coming till it's sitting in your lap
And is heavy
And is heavy and not easy to carry
And is *not* beautiful just 'cause it's new

'Love me or leave me and let me be lonely'

You Have Me Listening to Music Again...

You have me listening to music again
I turn off the blue tube
Listen to Coltrane in the nude
I snap my fingers
And stretch my legs
I think... I think.... I think
I'm rising for you
Climbing intertwined, love-making trees
To the top
And I pick and peel a passion fruit
And burst the pulp between my teeth
And roll the tart-sweet against my tongue
And think about the next rung of our "us" ...
Or, of your you...
Or whatever...whatever...whatever...
You've got me tapping my feet against the open, sleeping trees
And bending at the knees
To tell God all about your smile.

Stuttering/Speechless

His kiss...I...
My lips...
His kiss...I ...
My face...
Like spread out Roses
Busted cherry tomatoes...my face
Him...He...He makes me...
I am...hungry.
Famished/ Craving your face
I am missing
Your face
I am wishing I was kissing
Your face.
You...
Your face...
You...you...you are settling at the sharp turn
At the part of my mind that
Tells my heart
What to do.

Naming Ceremony

He calls me Wonderful.
Wonderful.
He calls me Wonderful.
Me
Belly full of wonder.

By Heart

He says he can see my bass with his eyes closed
Knows the deepest parts of me
Eyes closed.
Fingers posed to show me
How he can press music out of me...
Symphony
With his eyes closed and only his hands in motion.
Showing me how he makes this music by heart.
Because he has thought of me often and
Because practice makes more perfect than
Speech...
He plays me
Without looking.

Naming Ceremony II

I am already wanting to call you *Baby*...
Eyes...
Smile....
Teeth...
Something.
Something...
I am wanting to give you a name.
I am wanting to name you, so you know *that's* where it is.
That's where we are with this...at the nick- naming stage...
At the claiming stage, where you get to be a little more mine than you had been before.

Pen-less Poet

I am wanting to understand how he got to be this way
Telling me poetry without paper and pen
Without knowing it,
He is always making poems for me...
About me...
To me.
And I'm wanting to know,
How he got to be
So like walking Love.

Willing Addict

He wants me to be his addiction.
Also, he organizes/ outlines/ numbers,
The beautiful things he thinks about me...
Out loud...
Like this:
"Two things:
1. I want you to be my addiction.
2. *Everything* about you is amazing."

And I have interpreted this to mean,
He wants to plummet into his need for me...
And also is not easily bored with me...

And this pair of thoughts he shares,
Leaves me...
Hopeful

Traffic Light

We sat through the green, yellow, red
Green
Yellow
Red
We sat through the going
The slowing
The stops.
We talked.
We spoke to one another through the waiting and the stopping
We spoke to one another and we were existing together
In the midst of every stage of movement.
We were slowing
Stopping
Greening
Meaning we were moving forward
Toward the best, most exciting places
We were placing our faces against our own hands
Trying to hide the dents left in our cheeks,
From how Happy, had crashed carelessly
Into us.

Under Street Lights

We were holding each other under street lights.
We were lovely on lips and
Just around hips.
We were warm and relaxing about the spring we were feeling
We were noticing stubborn hills of leftover blizzard snow
And thinking how funny it was.
Leftover snow, refusing to melt,
While *we* were determined to puddle....
Determined to leave pavement slippery.
Soaking up warmth
Soaking...
We were soaking without rain
We were soaking and
Sticking to each other...
And separation
Was surgery
Took time and eventual consent
Took everything to walk home after kissing the frost away
Recognizing, that our Together
Was more marvelous than Apart.

Better

He makes me want to be a better person
Makes me want to be this Wonderful that he keeps calling me
He's calling me Wonderful.
I want to be all my potential
And stretch the possibilities beyond that too.
I want to master my goals after the meeting of them
Transform my words to actions after speaking them
I want to be someone he can be proud of
I want to be the one he speaks out loud about, to other cared about folks.

Restraint

We are not ready to place the words out loud in our air
And neither of us can tell time about this
I have decided that it will wait.
Out loud words will wait
Till we are bursting at the seams
With what these words mean.
They will wait
Till they're screaming through our pores and
Us can't take it no more....
We will hold words in our cheeks
Till the feeling leaks out of the side of our mouths
We are learning a beautiful patience about the UFO's
In our bellies
We are, about all things, taking steps
And slowly
We are baby walking
And the eager is smeared on our faces
And we can't hide
And won't forget
To let loose the feelings
When our chains of restraint are no longer enough
To hold the love words back.

His Hands

He wants to build and reside at my smile
Wants to live on my lips and build happy there
He wants to inhabit my joy
And that's beautiful to me
He is always speaking about the roughness
Of his hands
From the construction
Apologies for the roughness of his hands
His sometimes sandpaper hands
Sloughing away the old parts of me
And uncovering softer, more excellent places
I must remember to tell him to never apologize
For the hands
That make my heart better...

Breathing

I love him so hard and must remind myself to focus
Must remind myself of the rest of the world sometimes
Because I am often seeing only him and
Wanting to smell of his hug.
He leaves his scent on me
And I am breathing that much deeper
Air so much sweeter
I am opening my nose to the scent of this Love
And I am living so much better from all the
Breathing.

Journey to Healing

We escort each other through life
And journey through personalities and
Pasts and presents
We find the broken spots on hearts
And see them finally
Sutured.
We journey
Walk
Walk
Run
Run
To our mo' better future.

Hoarders

She and I
That lady and me
We have discovered that we are not spring cleaners
We are keepers, not always kept, but
Always keeping
We are holding onto history and
Old exams and birthday cards
We do not deny ourselves the dreams we dream about the past.
We put aside or put away, but
We pick back up again
We turn over yellowed paper and
Polo shirts
And pulsing poems in our hands
And it doesn't matter at all that these things are not of
Now
Doesn't matter that there are *new* poems
About new hearts
And white sheets of paper
With no hints /tints of any shade of yellow or brown
We are pack rats about our loves
And we are not 'shamed
We are smiling and laughing at us
And all our stuff
All our stuff making neatness almost impossible
We are not caring about oddities
And we are not garage selling

Or trash feeding
We are keeping and keeping and keeping the past
And still very faithful to our
Present.

Crazy

I have decided that this word:
"Crazy,"
Deserves closer inspection.
It is delegated to all things that cannot be understood,
Or described with other, more accurate words, at the moment.
Like when somebody tells you about a most bizarre day/evening circumstance
We tersely reply:
"Man, that's crazy."
Or it is the word given for folks who speak to unidentified persons or things.
No cellphone or musical playing device in sight...
Just them and their moving lips.
This misunderstood communication, inspires fear and fleeing by bystanders.

Or...

Like... love.
When it is so potent and making you.
When Love is making *you*
And you are smiling ...by yourself ... in public.
And not really worrying about what the people may think about your smile
With no joke or hilarious circumstance to justify it
Just smiling with *all* your teeth

By yourself
In public
And you don't care enough about the public diagnosis of your
Condition.
You are unashamedly teeth-showing.
You have dived into the thing,
And the depth has left you drunk and soaking
And not thinking about swimming to shore at all
You are just waiting/wading on more and more love and
Enjoying being this particular brand of insane.

Lovely Again

We were lovely again
And my doubt has dissipated.
We were wading in uncharted oceans of us
And we were breathing...I mean like...we were taking breath seriously
And not like a play thing
Breeeeaaaathing....
And wasting nothing.
We were ocean waving with the anticipating each other.
This strong young brother has me wanting...
Wanting .... wanting.... wanting.
And feeling like I'm needing
And more and more I am having trouble differentiating
Between the need and the want
I am not seeing the one different from the other
I am just knowing there is an urgency in the movement between us
We are moving like emergency
His lips are soothing places on me like fresh cut aloe on a burn
We are both the remedy *and* the reason...
We are the fire and the waters ... both.

Tears for You

Do you find them lovely?
Do you find it lovely?
Magical, maybe,
How easily I make
Ocean on my face for you?

Manipulation

Love is playdoughing me
Moving me around
Mushing and mashing me
Changing the shape of me like...
Like I don't have bones...
And then I get scared...
Where are my bones?
The love has me on a frantic search for my
Skeleton.

Reminder

I have to remind myself about myself
My life
What I taste like
Without additional preservatives
Without added, artificial flavoring
What do I taste like *without* the love?
Can I preserve the flavor of me
When love is boiling my insides
Making all things tender?
Me: easier to bite through
Just cause I like dude
And he makes me easier to bite through
Makes me reassess
All the teeth
I peep
When he
Smiles.

Skin

I am a person of feelings
And dreams of future things.
I am the strongest desire for muscles
And soft places,
Both my own.
I am often fearful
And sometimes crazy
(Making me fear ...less.)
I am maybe...
Paranoid...
Worried often about my skin
When it pimples or breaks
Or gives up on me,
Making my, barely there, bones
Visible
I must get back to the laughing part of me.
That kite-flying, carefree me...
That me, who is laughing too hard,
And smiling too easily
To care
About my broken
Skin.

Longing

Longing is the place on your back
You can't reach in the shower
By yourself
Or
The parts of you
You *can* reach,
But it's nicer with my help.

Lashes

Your lashes are too long.
They mock me.
Make me wrap my mauve mind
Around thoughts of you.
And well that ain't fair
Makes me want to breathe you in...
And well damn...
That ain't air.

It's There

After much debate with myself,
I tell you,
I love you.
Whether you feel you need it or not,
It's there.
Persistent.
Mixing with oxygen and clouds
Whether you breathe it in or not
It is there like handprints and scribbled nicknames
And declarations of crush in wet concrete
Dried now and permanent.
Whether you need it or not
It's there.
Like that extra pair of underwear
In every suitcase you've ever packed
When traveling away to palm trees and sun
It's there
In working condition
If you need it or don't
If you don't but
Crave it anyway
It's there
It's there with or without
Your permission
The love is sitting here with me
And in between the distance of our long ago....
Far away...us.

And if you trip and fall anywhere
Or don't trip and just fall
It will be there for you to fall on
Or in.
It's there at the parts of your back you can't get to
It's in between the curl of your lip
Whether you smile or sneer or spit
It's sitting right there
In the darkest brown part of your eyes
Playing peek-a-boo with the twinkle there
Whether you need it or not
Or whatever else
No pressure
Just presence
It's there.

Found Out

So at last
I'm found out.
There is *still* love.
And I still remember the love words
That were always for him
No matter how well I'd try to hide him
Behind nameless, gendered articles...
Normal pronouns
He was always "him" and "he"
I covered him in anonymity.
But he is always peeking out
And I see him
And pretend I don't
Because he changes the tone of my
Face flesh
And I don't match anymore
And I'm supposed to be grown up
Grown up, and over him
Supposed to have climbed up and over him
Or at least...
I'm tall
If not grown up...
Certainly tall.
I'm so tall, I thought I was taller than love thoughts of him...
I'm not.
And he knows
He's been hiding in my poetry all along.

The Words

I have built synonyms around the words I wish to say to him.
I have told him paragraphs and metaphors in place of the words.
I have clothed him in kisses 'cause it's cold outside.
I have hugged him and rubbed him and
Memorized the dips and climbs of him...
I have tasted his skin and been satisfied.
I have housed him in my hips
And dipped deep where the waves are...
Where the craves are...
I have tickled him that I might have the laughter I love.
I have stroked his beard in deep thought and
I often dive in his eyes when I have no words.
I have sighed into his neck
And eaten his breath
And wanted to know his life,
His dreams,
His hopes,
His happy.
I woke up and reached across my sheets wanting;
And it was not for moan, or arched back, or night rhythm that I ached.
This morning's ache was about him in his all-ness,
With no parts left out or behind.
I hungered to wake to the sight of him...
And this is new to me...
And this means the words I *want* to say
The words I want to say, but save instead...

Everything

My tongue is bending and flicking and rolling over r's
To say in all languages and in however many ways...
I love you
I love you with curry, ginger, wasabi, honey, and you...
On my tongue
I tell you in any flavor...
However you'd like it...
Sugar or spice it...
It's yours for the taking, baking, frying, sighing, stripping, teasing, marinade-ing, Serenading...
do/re/me/so/fah/ into this loving thing...
This kiss and hugging thing...
So far into you...
I have passed mile markers
So far into you....
I couldn't drive no more
Cause there were oceans
So I flew
I wrote a rap-ture for the heart capture and was taken up into the sky so high
You leave my eyes read...
My mind...read...
My face...red.
You leave me loved...and assured...
Loved *and* assured
And okay about my pre-kindergarten selfishness
Yes, you are mine and nobody else-eses....

You are the most beautiful jaw... and lips....and fingertips...
And two hour trips
Just to bring me Dayquil and kiss.
You are singing songs off key
And unlocking things
I didn't know I keep.
You are reading the books off my bookshelves
And sending me jamming Def Poets
Because you want to know me better...
And give me what I like...
Well, *you* are what I like...and love...
You are like Costco's dude...
I have found everything I need
In you.

Time Enough

He is wanting of her
Wanting of her so much
He is wanting all her
Clocks and watches
He is always hungry for her time
And cannot be satisfied.

The First Time

Broken berry cherry ...cherry...
"Pop"
Busted, busted love
Flowed out and over
Crusted

Attempt at Excavation

I run, run
Swallow sheets and
Blankets of dreams and nightmares
Posing the lips into angry positions
Equated anger with strength ...
Turns out they are not the same
All is confusion.
Getting tired of trying to sort them out...
The makings of my madness...
They eat me...
The sheets
The blankets
The pillows
The pills
The purple, purple, purple blood water
I swallow me
He...he...he...he...
He's funny
Maker of jokes of me
Poking me in the face
Poking my secret place in public
It's a joke.
He throws out the punk lines
She falls for it
Falls for he
Backwards/ forwards...
Breaks her knees wide open and laughs

At her broken funny bones
He laughs between her
Moan cry groans
Finds her feelings funny
Finds her feelings funny
So he plays with them
Rolls them around in his calloused hands
Gets scared when he finds his hands getting soft
Because he doesn't understand the
Steel of soft...
The strength of her tears/ her screams
All along he was softening against the pressure of her
dreams
She was tearing his hips at the seams and making him use
his mind
She was rising against his chest
Working up the nerves to stretch her spinal cord
To meet him at the place where his heart was supposed to
be
She snatched frantically
At the layers of him that had nothing to do with anything
more than
Appearance
Trying to get to where his heart was .... supposedly...
She took hold and tore away at the bullshit parts
Scraped up the whitewash
And he smiled sideways...
Amused by her efforts
Diligent she/ diligent she/ she diligently

Pulled away/ tore away
Ripped away/ dug into/ dug into
Tore…tore …snatched at/ pulled
Dug into/ dug into
God she made a mess of his layers
She did
Tore till tired/ tore till tired/ tired/tired
Till the tears were too much…
Dug into…till too damn tired…
And …and…and…
Love is her God
And she finds she can't worship here…
Dug into…the dream… ripped up all seams and …and…
Can't sing hymns about him heart
Him won't give not 10%
She…she…she…
Dug into…. dug…into…and…
Love is her God
And she finds she can't worship here
Finds after all her digging…
He was not Love, and the worship had been in vain.

Deadline

Feeling lonely
Concerned about the time and my heart
Concerned about tick tock
Ba-boom, ba-boom
Tick- tock
Concerned time is passing
I'm gaining years
Feeling like there's a deadline on
Finding a forever love
And I'm going to miss it.

Substitute

He sent a picture of his tongue
Reaching out to me
It was not a sufficient substitute for conversation.

California Closets

California closets are keeping
My foolish folded
And my sadness sorted
All of the unwelcomed
Insanity
Is neatly kept.

You Rock my World

You rock my world and
I am stoned
You rock my world
I fall asleep easy with you
You rock my world
I ease beneath the waves
And get to your depths
You're deep and I don't want to be saved
My arms are up in adoration and surrender
You rock my world
I throw myself into you and you hold me
And move me over the shock of electric guitar
You rock my world
And my lands and oceans are shifted and I cannot tell
If I'm in Asia, Africa, or Australia
All I know is that *I am*
And you are
Rocking the hell out of my world.

Intelligent

He's bright
I'm drenched
In effervescence

The Way He Loved Her

He loved her in a way that
Frightened the weak of heart
He loved her with a love that stained sidewalks and sides of city buildings
The love left an aroma that stayed
For days
And left unsuspecting persons
High off the wind

The love ripped and strained through the muscles of his arms,
Which were like winter midnight
The love pushed out through his fingertips and she was touched
And there was precipitation at eyes
Or thighs
Or both.

The love bent between their differences
And they fit
And fold
And stretch
Arm strong
In their hugs
He loved her in howl and scream
That unsettled those who did not know it was him
Howling at her
In worship

He loved her to the sweating point
And she wiped his brow with the edge of her hands
He loved her against the hurt of the world
And wept when he could not
And there were times when
He could not

He smiles when he sees that she is strong
And will be okay
Even when *he* can't make it that way

He loved her to insanity
Talked to himself about the love in or outside of rhyme
Laughed in silent moments
And shook his head at memories
Of Her

He buried his face in her and swallowed her scent
And could not be sober
She laughed at the drooping of his eyes,
Heavy with the ecstasy
Weighing down his lids

She said "You're beautiful...you're beautiful"
He said "I am a river...the beauty is you."

He loved with a love that broke the
Yuck moments of life
He loved her to trembling
Loved her to laughter
Loved her to life.

Scars

She is fascinated by these people without scars
Uninterrupted skin stretched against muscle.
Scars frequent her own skin
Scars from falls, from bites, scratches,
Burns
Scrapes
Passion
How is it that there are those without this?
Without these...
Life marks.

I.

And love is her body heat
Melting his cool
He will be geek for her
And love it.

II.

He will eat grapes out of her
Hand
And will be healthy off of the love
He will bite her arm knowing
She is sweet
And also good for him.

III.

The love left him leaned over and heavy
He could not stay standing
For the strength of the love…
The love that was scratching his back and
Wiping his forehead of the sweat,
That was her fault.

Allegory of the Cave

I have climbed out of the cave
And seen sunlight
I have seen sunlight and now understand that
The puppeteers were lying
The shadows are not
Reality
They are perpetrators of The Real.
I have broken out of the shackles and
Have ceased calling them bracelets.
Captivity's accessories no longer hold me.
I now know...the fire is *not* the sun
It's just an Imitator
And you are not Love
You are fuck,
In the dark with fire.
You are a liar,
Who looks bigger, and more important, in the dark...
With the fires lit...
In the distance.
I was in love with the shadow of you
Which explains, why I was never able
To hold you.

Anonymous

The night was hiding her well
And he would fuck her
Anonymously
And not touch her
And not kiss her
And not eat her
And not lick her
And cup his head deep down ...
Through her
And come up with more than enough
Of what he needed.

Easy

She was easy
To manipulate
She was a one size fits all
Glove
And he and him and him too
Had a hand in her
Slow demise
He could say "I need…"
And she would say
"I have"
Or
"Can find…"
Or…
"Will get…and it's yours…"
And he could say "Lay down 'cause it makes me feel nice…"
And she would.
And he may never converse with her lips
But he would tear her hips
Apart
And *still* not split her open enough
To see her heart
And kiss her head.
He could say,
"I want"
And she would hear…
"I need"

And for the sake of necessity,
He would have his want
That would take all she had to give...
She felt she *had* to give
Cause he said,
"You are of lovely"
And she said, "You love me?"
And he quickly clarified.
And she sighed, but was still
Satisfied with the substitute
Settling
Settling
Settling six feet deep
In artificially flavored words
And prepacked and widely distributed dialogue.
He knew which words to choose
And where to place them
So she'd find them
Exquisite.

Prayer: I come to you

I come to you
I come to you with the broken pieces...
The soaked pieces...
I come to you
Move my purple
Deep purple
Red, blue explosion
Wine-stained lips against your ear
I say nothing
I come to you
Mute motions against your open ear
I destroy the sobriety of your mind
With the moving of my broken mouth
Moving against your ear
Breaking off into sound behind your eyes
Don't cry.
Don't cry.
Just listen
I come to you.
I come to you
Because
I've broken my skin...again and
I'm still afraid of time
I come to You...
Fix me.

Relapse

Relapse

We laugh again
Reach deep into each other's bellies and
Pull out chuckle and giggle
We slide in between each other's teeth when we're caught smiling there
He rubs me back to laugh with him
and we watch us revive to some remixed form of we
Again
We wrap lips around skies
And coil tongues around storms
Again we breathe in stories
Hold them in our mouths and
Release them
Again
And in between memories of morning on my lips
He finds all my voice and
Pulls verbose silence from the inside of my cheeks
Holds up my mind with his right hand and tastes my thoughts when they
Stream down his fingertips
And we dissolve an entire world with a moment
And we breathe a new one into being
And for a little while I forget that he said he's gotta settle down
And that that has nothing to do with me
For that small tear in time I find myself making and remaking memory

Beneath the sun and smells of burning peaches
I let him hold me apart and rewire ventricles
And other means of transporting life in me
and I try to remind myself not to be conquered
He takes all of me and all my biography
And even though I'd outgrown it
I take and bend love back into me
Push down with my knee
Close my eyes and seal it tight
Make sure it doesn't pop open
Hope it's not too heavy to hold onto
Place it in the overhead compartment
And take it home
Upon arrival...I undo...unzip...unpack
Relapse.

In Darkness

His lips found mine and he drank
Sipped up the slur in my speech
Hand supporting the back of my jelly neck
As he mumbled against my lips and mine leaned against his
In darkness, he cups his hands in my lap
Thirsting for all of me
Holding me together and pulling me apart between my hips
And I am never still with him like this with me

In darkness, I breathe him in through lighted fires
I breathe him in black and brown and golden
And the part of his face where he is a man most, tickles me
But I'm too high above the simplest feelings to laugh
So I smile
Lazy
Eyes...lazy
Lazy 'cause all the rest of me is working so hard to keep it together
As he pulls me apart
Trying to get inside the soft, vulnerable parts of me
Me giving way beneath his touch, so light but heavy
And it's hard for me to keep it together

In darkness, he lays me down secretly
All to himself
Kept

Slips in beside me
He hides me
Beneath him
Pulls me in off of all four walls
Easy
Takes me from me and gives me back to me
Changed
Whispers his wishes between my breasts
And I beat him with my heart
And bruise the edges of his mind
Bruise and bend him with the beneath me parts
For wanting and wishing what could only be whispered
In darkness

In darkness, he smoothes out the dizziness of my mind
In slow motion, he helps ease the intoxication
Drowns me in newness
And I breathe in Enlightenment
He wraps me in my own amazement of this us
Wraps me so tight till I don't remember the other us before this
Darkness
This darkness bringing everything to light
Unfolding mysteries and removing all the seams
And every part falls to the ground honest and basic and
Waiting
And I don't know how to put all of "us" back together like we were before

There's something different about the smooth of the silk and
The soft of the cotton
And I can't even bring myself to talk about
The colors

In darkness, we pick up crumbs and find constructed confections
And stick our tongues searchingly into the cavities

In darkness, a kiss is alarm clock and I wake from years of sleep
Here beneath the lack of luminescence I lose my voice
And my first words after I wipe me of this birth,
Are nonsense.
He took me and moved me beneath, above and in and
Out of truth
Fresh out of the flames of his fought feelings

In darkness, I found the light towards the end of the tunnel
And fell off the rusted tracks I'd been traveling on
In darkness, I find me
Falling awake painfully.

Glutton

I am a glutton
May not be hungry at all
But once I get a taste…
Just a taste of something good
I stick my hands in it and serve it to my mouth…
unapologetically…
Gluttonous 'bout everything
This…my emotions…
My love…
Even when it begins to hurt
I partake till I'm drowsy off it all.
Till I'm good for nothing but sleep.

Something Sweet

I am wanting something of sweet
Without an attack on my heart
I am wanting to digest something
Lovely
And not have to amputate parts of myself in the process.

Dentist

Do it sweet style
Like ...give me
Cavities
Off the loving
I want
To need
To see the dentist please.

Remodel your Mind

Read by the light of me
And expand your mind
'Til I can fit in there
That would be nice and also, perhaps
Life-saving.

Massage My Mind

Massage my mind
Will you... pour oil down the
Highways of my hair
And massage my mind?
Massage my mind
And find the release
Enlightening.

Honest

Tell me words of truth or be silent
Tell me true things
Or be mute
And speak to me with your hands.
Give me truth or nothing at all
Give me You
No Frills
No Frills
Give me you with no extra trimmings
Or anything that will confuse me or
Fool me into thinking you are not you.
Give me real
Give me real and not
Pinocchio
Don't poke me with the length of your nose
Give me real
True
There is magic
In the Honest
Give me that.

Flower Words

I think I have tired of spoken flowers
Don't give me flower words
That didn't come from
Deep digging and dirty hands
And burning sun
And pouring rain.
Don't forget the thorns
And bee-butt bites
Don't give me part...
Give me all or nothing.
Don't promise me springtime
When there's snow on the ground
Just 'cause it's the warmest Jersey winter night yet...
Tell me real
Tell me there is snow
And warmth
Both
And it fools you.
Don't promise me what you cannot give
Or grow...
I don't want it
At all.

Wings

He says, "I won't necessarily stay…"
With heat in her cheeks and rushed thought-words
She says,
"Me neither…not stuck…
Not frozen…
No…me neither…
I'm about wings
And what wings do
If you help them to…
I'm about that.
I could fly too."
He does not know that his words were the magic
That made her grow wings that she did not mean.

Needwanting

I am finding it difficult at times to handle myself.
I am often wanting to rock my hips against strength
And feel like I've birthed muscle.
Pulsing...pulsing

I miss the meeting of life and life.....
Blood rushing,
Stretching skin to fit desire
Purposeful slipping/sliding into place...
Finding space to move inside need and satisfy want
And it's nice
Not to worry about pinpointing the difference.
Nice to focus on finding both need and want
Separately or together ...

Most often confusing the two
So that it no longer matters about the difference...
Whichever...
Feeling or fact...
Need or want
It matters not
There is no hierarchy...
Only heat.

Sunbit (Just before Winter)

The warmth is satisfying me
I am burning/toasting/browning/ blackening...
The sun is eating me
And her tongue is fire
And fire
And mo' fire
And I feel delicious for being tasted
Licked slow
All over
And then bitten into
And there is juice.
And it is from me...
And the sun gets swollen
And bursts and
Shards of her scatter
Everywhere
And my skin releases tears...
I loved her.

Sun Child

The sun makes me giddy
And I run to her
Laughing and eager
With sweat
On my thighs.

Dimples

Sitting here looking out glass window, like glass door, like glass wall
Watching people walk
People laugh
People smile…
Watching other people watch people walk
People laugh
People smile sometimes…
Then…I see him.
He is not "people"
Not even "other people"
He…is *HIM*….
He is the him I want to be mine…
But he…is with her…
She used to be "people"
Sometimes "other people"
Why, she was them till she was with him

Now he and she
Yes, him and her…are *they*
And they are sitting out there beyond the dividing of this
Glass window, like glass door, like glass wall
They are sitting out there beyond me sitting in this chair
Watching people walk
People laugh
People smile sometimes…
And then I realize how …the sun shines on him

Like my eyes on him
Like my love...on...him
And when she is gone like the wind...
He comes in
Through the glass revolving doors
Never open
Never shut
Taking in what they put out and putting out what they took in
He sits in front of me
Blocking...my...view
But I don't mind
Now I'll watch him
Watch him smile
Making his cheeks collapse
Just a little...in the middle...into dimple
Dimple where I press my lips into soft kiss
making him smile sunshine on me again
Like his eyes on me again
Like his love on me...again

And when he waves her over here...
I brace myself...
Grace myself
Force myself to prepare myself to say.... "hello"
And then he tells me that she is not the she I thought her to be ...
No...she...is his SISTER....

So now my lips spread out smiled and my cheeks collapse into dimple...
For now she is "people"
Sometimes "other people"
She is them...
And he is him...and I am me...and we?
Shoooooot ... we are US...

He Comes to Me Quietly

He comes to me quietly
A whispered hand against my belly
A rustling of slow purposed
Movement
(Turned to me)
What does he say?
I feel like something is said...
But I can't place words or sound at all.
Only this quiet...
Not like a secret...
Like a wish.
Like a wish that won't come out of sound
Only with sleeping eyes
And soft, deep breath.
He comes to me quietly...
A whispered touch,
A series of conversations I never hear, but understand...
Quietly thorough and complete sentences
And stanzas
And songs
And he is holding me
Together.
He is making things make sense.
He is not taking and leaving
He is giving and sharing and
Holding

Not a smothering, possessive hold
He is laying his arm around my waist lightly
And I am knowing
That he's there.

Digestion

You see these eyes that ate you?
Watch my face for the digestion
How the pieces of you curl my lips
And make my teeth naked.
See...see...see...
What you've done...what you do to me?
I am trying to avoid gluttony...
Because I've read that it's a sin.
And I'm not religious, but I care
About heaven
Or You...
(Tasting like streets of chocolate covered gold)
I bite...nibble...lick.... swallow
In slow satisfaction
I take my time
Tasting your life.

Journey Out of Mind

And your fingers take flight
And run insanity around the complexity
Of my hips
Down the slope of my legs
Run insanity
Cleverly between the hidden and open parts of my mind
Run crazy
Along my heart
Crazy
Crazy that makes so much sense,
If you understand that crazy
Is often an opinion and only sometimes
A fact.

Since Yesterday

I've loved you since yesterday.
It's been 12 hours.
I've loved you...
And have not slept.

Pagefright

Feeling like an intruder
Like an imposter
Like I don't really belong
Like my depth is not enough
And the people will know and point
And be pleased
With their discovery
Me…fool's gold
Cracker Jack prize
In the way of what is really wanted.

But no matter the thoughts of the audience…
This is mine.
This art.
The words.
The worlds I speak into memory and imagination
They are mine.
I made them.

I can't deny the existence of my fear.
It too is mine.
I'm scared
Scared…
Shivering in the corner sometimes
In awe of the greatness that is before me, beside me, above me…

The words of the writing warriors who have emerged
victorious before me, beside me, above me..
Leaving me, sometimes, feeling inadequate.
Wondering if I've taken my words to a deep enough depth,
To make them treasure.

Claustrophobia

Here there is no space for a cocky swagger
My hips have no room for full sway
And if I bump my confidence
Against waiting chairs
The dim lights will tell on me and
The silent shadows will laugh at me.
In the small space that draws me into revelations and leaves me open to opinions,
I find myself gasping for air and hoping I will be given enough space
To be.

Mother and Son

She is pointing out life
Says, "Look at this world baby..."
And
"Baby, I didn't make this world...
Just brought you to it
And will often want to ...
Will often... *Need* to...
Protect you from it."
She pinpoints the beautiful parts
And says, "Hey baby, look...open your eyes to
This part...see...
The lovely."
He smiles and points and takes a try at
Wrapping language around it all.
He holds three of her fingers
And she smiles at the best magic she made.

If only you knew

If only you knew
How much I do...
Do love you...
You'd probably pee in your pants
And cry
If you knew
How much I loved you...
Then.
When loving came easy
'Cause my heart was whole
Now, my heart's a hole,
That men better than you
Fall through
Good job...
Thanks.

He

You are the "he" of half of my poetry.
The anonymous male person
Playing on my pages
Playing with blood
And smearing it on walls.
Playing with my face
Having much to do with how my lips
Pose
Pushing up my chin
Like you care about my pride.
Playing
Playing with my mental and
Heart space
And now I've made you famous
On my pages.

Horror Story

He is a vampire
He never warned me in conversation
Never really did admit to it
But he is a vampire
And it all makes sense now
How he would not see me in daylight
How the Sun's arms frightened him
And he would only see me
When she'd gone.
He's a vampire
And it makes sense now,
How he sucked life from me
And laughed
It makes sense now
Those things he had said about sunshine and
His refusal to hold me in the morning…
Turns out the cherry kool-aid stain was really
Blood at the corners of his lips
The red in my back…
The holes where my heart used to be…
The cuts in my calves…
The delay in my journey
My eternally unsatisfied yearning
It makes sense now
He was a vampire
Who believed he had an eternity to decide
Whether or not to love me.

Advice

"Run...run...
Run and stop...
Eating,"
He said,
To her whom he'd fucked
Several times
"Run, and don't eat,"
He said to she who had sat in his lap
And rocked him
Into insanity
He had held her love handles
And found them convenient
When he supped at the meeting of her thighs
He bit the dimples, the ripples of her skin
And grabbed handfuls of her ass
And loved it.
And now...
Now he says, "You should run or something....and...
Don't eat."
He who she tired in horizontal strides...
He said, "Run and don't eat..."
He who she'd waited for
30 minutes...40 minutes...an hour...
On several December nights on 34th St.
He who apologized a thousand times
For being late...again.
Him who she shook her head about

He who had fucked her when she had the flu
And hadn't bothered to warm her...
This "he" with the name she did not like.
With the place... (The suffocating room) ...
She did not like.
He whose words came out in a voice
She did not find musical or beautiful...
He... wanted her to be half of herself and
Hungry.
Half herself and hungry
And fucked
A thousand times
With no release
On a New York night.
He said run.
He said run.
He *said* run.
He....
Had no idea
She'd run so fast
And far.

Getting Over

There has got to be a more appropriate term
Than: "Getting Over" him
"Getting over" is a geographically incorrect statement
A misunderstanding of placement
His location is not Below.
He's inside of me.
Meaning he and my insides reside together
He and my kidney, my liver, my heart
Shared residence
My soul and he were roommates
My bones and he shared wall space.
There is not a getting over
There is the excavation process.
It is major surgery
Amputation.
A most excruciating relocation.
"Getting Over" is a term that misrepresents
The Depth.

Recovery and Relapse

How will I learn to tell him,
About his smile
About his shoulders
About the music he makes
With his mouth
About the way I dream him
Into the newly found strength of my arms
And am satisfied to the sleeping point.
I wish for him to translate me into his language
And speak me
Fluently
With a slight accent.
I'd like him to speak me with pepper on his breath
And sweat at the back of his neck
I'd love him to like how I lose my balance
With the disagreeing weights of my thoughts.
I'd allow him to bow
At the poetry of my hips.
I'd lead him to the liquor of love
That I've stored for such a time as this.
You must understand that the presence of his hands
Increases my heartbeat
That the presence of his breath
Beneath my shoulder blades
Blows my cover
And I am naked
And he sees my heart's ankles

And I blush through my brown
He gets through my brown
He gets in and around my inside places
And makes it just a little easier

To believe again.

Into the Air

Her strength is the most beautiful thing I've ever seen
She makes me think she loves me
When she carries herself over herself...
Lifts herself over herself and doesn't bend...
She makes me want to love her
Let her carry me
Or maybe help *me* carry me
Assist me with the lifting of myself.

She is beautiful
How she bends and pulls in and at the air
And the air makes room for how she feels
How she emotions through the clouds
Clouds thicker than they look...
And she moves through and bites a piece of heaven and chews
And the digestion is clear blue water rain
Clean ...renew...
Is...morning dew
And my feet get wet.

She is so strength
So fight
She dances to freedom speeches and moments of silence
She stands so strong and tall
So feel
So emotion
She is so fire

So tree
And damned if her roots don't grow in me
Through me
And I style my branches every morning

Her eyes never waver
They search/seek/ find and demand more…
And I feel like she could make me love her
Make me swim against the tide
Fierce and determined
Swim against the waves and bathe in my determination
My persistence
My stubborn love so deep
Deep like the paths in her flesh where she is muscle
Deep like the streams of her body's libation
Poured in remembrance of her dance/interpretation of life
And I bite down the quiver in my lips
Stopping the ballet of my mouth
When she stares at or above
Or to either side of me

Yes she…she is beautiful
And with every rise and fall of her my chest follows
She is the
Pound Pound
Knock Knock
Of my heart against my chest, where she lay her head to rest
Beautiful.

be you...even in love

Don't forget yourself...
Even in love
Don't let love leave you drunk with the sweet ambrosia that strips memory and
Leaves you without mind pictures of yourself
Leaves you with so many thoughts of an "us" that you forget who *you* were
Before the "we"
Be you...because that is where love began
Love began with you being You...
And he/she loved the you that you were so well
And your individuality
Was fire for a butterfly's evening cousin
Be the fire of yourself...
Let them love you for that
Like you love them for their selfhood...
It is not selfish to be yourself...
It is honest
And it is your life requirement

Be you and see the love in that

Tried Being an Ocean

I wanted to write about a cause or an issue
I wanted to be deep and write about war and blood-covered soccer balls and
Misunderstood turbans...
Wanted to feed paper ink about
The children with maggot pregnancy...and cinnamon stick limbs
Wanted to pencil in some poetic notes
About lost and/or miscounted votes (somehow, often in black and brown neighborhoods)
Wanted to marry some verbs and subjects
About the apathetic public
I really wanted to spray paint a red, blue, and purple paragraph
About the teams with guns calling themselves thugs and
I wanted to write about women's rights to make choices
...still
I thought about too many news reports that made my neck hurt for shaking my head
And wanted to pen police with faulty vision into prison
So there is no more mistaking wallets, or hands, or... whatever for a gun
I wanted to write unity around this great divide we call earth
Wanted to erase hurt and re-write it to look more like laughing children
And meant hugs....all around...for free....whenever...

But no matter how I angled my writing device...
Tried it once, twice,
Three times this lady could not
Be deep at quite the right depth...because no matter how hard I try
All I can write about
Is love.

Lesson

I learned something of great value today.
One's love for another is divine.
Love can be salvation if you allow her to be.
Today love caressed someone's wrists
And so a knife did not.
Out of love, a fist bloomed and birthed a hand that massaged a heart back to life.
The love...the love... the love...
The love kidnapped my frown lines
And my lips couldn't be happier.
Taste it.
It will fill you
And pull you into satisfied
And rub you down to content
And hold you...together.

Discovery: Treasure After All

There is something of the lovely
In liking who you be and how you are
There is something of the amazing
In looking into your own mind
And discovering treasure there
I discovered my wealth
And filled my pockets with my thoughts...
I bit into my books
And digested the journeys of a thousand authors and found myself changed
I found myself in love
With the way my mind works
And the way my lips hold the loveliest of words.
The summer came
And brought me another year between her teeth and I took it
And stretched it over my skin
And the bold in me broke out,
A wild thing....
And things will never be the same again...

Prayer

May I always have love
Even if it doesn't last
Even if it's fragile
And I bump into heartache again ("Hello")
May I always fall into some love
May I always be left with some pieces...
Some remnants
Some staying memories
For even when it's been over...
Every time it's been over
Every time...
Even when it's just been my imagination all along,
I'm always left with the words.
I'm always left with all the colors of the love
I'm always left with something to paint my pages with.

CPSIA information can be obtained
at www.ICGtesting.com
Printed in the USA
BVHW060846240921
617110BV00004B/6